Keep Walking!

Walk With Me

*Daily Wisdom From the Sharp Mind
(and Sometimes Tongue) of Derek Triplett*

Published by: 3DTrip Publishing

www.derektriplett.com

Trademarks

First Edition, December 2016

Contact the Author

Connect with **Derek Triplett** at
booking@derektriplett.com

Visit his Website at
www.derektriplett.com
Derek Triplett
dtrip@derektriplett.com

DEDICATIONS:

To my Dad who taught me to think. To my Mom who showed me how to love.

To the members of Family of Hope who have embraced so many of my ideals.

Thanks to the DTM/3D Trip team.

Special thanks to my daughter, Destanni for compiling the quotes and to Byrdology for their creative excellence.

DEREK T. TRIPLETT

Derek T. Triplett is a speaker, writer, and change agent. He has over 26 years of experience in pastoral ministry and has served as a Bishop for over 18 years. He is a radio and television personality in Orlando, Florida.

He is a frequent guest speaker in churches, schools and conferences.

He is also the author of When I Became A Man: A Perspective on Manhood, Life and Relationships.

He is married and the father of two adult children and the stepfather of two.

You can reach him on his website

www.derektriplett.com

This book is designed to challenge you and stretch your thinking about your life and relationships.

Don't just read it but space has been provided for you to write down how the day's quote fits into your life and how you will apply it.

Make yourself accountable by telling someone important to you what you will do.

JANUARY

/01

Lift your hands. Be still. Wait.

/02

To what will you give your all this year? Will anything get your everything?

/03

Growth is when you can tell Satan, "I'm sorry. You must have confused me with someone who doesn't know any better. I don't listen to liars."

/04

Don't let a little rain stop you. Cross over.

/05

Some relationships were a mistake. Learn to treat them as such. Stop trying to fix what's meant to be eliminated.

/06

Relationships are work! Chillin is not. Choose the one you're ready for but don't try to mix the two.

/07

How much time do you have left to wish things were different? Your future is not in what you couldn't or didn't prevent. It's in how sincerely you can repent and what you and God can invent.

/08

The Christian church is in the business of transformation. Change is what we do.

/09

I can't be average today,

/10

The Holy Spirit must show us the difference between giving up and letting go,

---

/11

Try never to pull up flowers to make room for weeds.

/12

Know who you can work with. Know who you can play with. Know who you can pray with. Know what you can live with.

/13

Find a happy woman and make her happier. Stop trying to rescue or take advantage of the miserable.

/14

When it's time to change, CHANGE.

/15

It costs to be intentionally Christian without exception.

#letsgochurch

/16

There is no next Dr. Martin Luther King, Jr., but right NOW YOU can be one who loves, cares, and hurts enough to sacrifice for the greater good of your people.

/17

You got to know when to trust your heart and soul and when not to.

/18

Don't get an "A" with your friends and followers by always posting pics and statuses and get an "F" with your real friends and fam by rarely picking up the phone or spending time.

/19

WITH is a strong word. "I'm with…" is the beginning of a powerful sentence. That is why Satan loves to separate, cause division, and orchestrate bad connections. Together is better. Who ya with?

/20

Plenty of women can make your night. Find the one who makes your day after day after day after day…

/21

Discover, Determine, and/or Decide what you love. If it's right get to it. If it's wrong get delivered. Before and after deliverance, be disciplined.

/22

Humanity is God's greatest creation. Love is God's greatest gift. Hook up the two and you have something amazing!

/23

Before you decide to start decide to finish.

/24

Lord, please don't let me mistake a "not yet" for a "no". Don't want to quit on something I have to wait on. And don't let me ignore a "no" and take it for a "not yet". Don't want to be waiting in vain.

/25

Have the courage not to hesitate.

/26

If you're not a bride then something old, something new, and something borrowed all at the same time will eventually make someone blue.

/27

Don't try to manipulate the friend zone. And don't get manipulated in the friend zone.

/28

Make sure that what's important to you is actually important. Don't increase your investment in diminishing assets or definite liabilities.

/29

Sometimes the enemy attacks. Other times life happens. At times God is revealing or shaping your character or sharpening a skill. Whatever hits you and your life just trust Him at all times.

/30

You can't win if you are the most successful person at defeating you.

/31

Stop letting bad seed be sown in your good ground. You're allowing wasted space and potential contamination. Something good could be growing in that spot.

FEBRUARY

/01

You may never know what or why but as long as you know "you know who" you're going to be all right.

/02

Ladies and fellas, are you test-driving or joy riding? Is the car yours? Was it grand theft or carjacking?!

/03

Buying presents is not a proper substitute for constant absences. Make time for her.

/04

Some people know what they want. They are just trying to see if there is an easier way to get it.

/05

The Christian life is a rowboat, not a cruise ship. Exhausted people can't row. Get rest so you won't have to be rescued.

/06

This is the day I...

/07

What a trap!!!! When you're in the process, sometimes winning feels bad and losing feels good. Remember that both feelings are temporary.

/08

Don't pretend. Grow.

/09

You can't have "next" without "ex". There is old you have to let go to get the new.

/10

The only way to escape work and sacrifice in a relationship is to have a string of insignificant others. To have a true significant other you MAY have to work to get her, and you WILL have to work with her for both of you to be fulfilled. Find the relationship (not just the woman) that's worth the work.

/11

Live at full speed.

/12

Christianity is not Church. Don't just go to and work in...church. Go get and work on...LIFE.

#churchisgoodlifecanbebetter

/13

Challenge yourself and win the challenge.

/14

Some things shake us. Some things shape us. Some things sharpen us. Sometimes they can be the same thing.

/15

Never and Always are two of the biggest words in the English language. Be careful using them. They're almost always never true.

/16

If you live a lic to keep from being alone, the real you is still by his/herself.

/17

Remember "just chillin" is easier than real dating. Real dating is easier than marriage. Never confuse the three. The responsibilities and rewards are different. Know which one you're ready for.

/18

Frenemies have become acceptable, especially with our youth. WRONG. Don't hang out with people with enough hang-ups with you to hang you out to dry.

/19

The next ten years in America will require a different kind of Christian than the last ten. The kingdom is suffering real violence. Battles on multiple fronts. Get in shape to fight.

/20

Determine your standards. Define your boundaries. Develop your team. Deny yourself. Defeat your enemies.

/21

You will lose some battles, some things, and some people. Just don't lose your faith so you can begin to win again.

/22

Never allow the negative you hear to become the negative you speak. The mouth is more deadly than the ears.

/23

The beauty and benefit of true intimacy (I do not define true intimacy as sex) is you get to shARE who you ARE with another. If you have to be someone else in order to be with them, then it's not meant to be. You can and should improve. But improvement is not the same as the requirement to become something other than a better you.

/24

Ultimately love is a decision. If she accepts your love it's a privilege. If you accept her love it's a responsibility.

/25

Some people won't ask for help. Some people shouldn't have to.

/26

Why do we "tell our neighbor" so much stuff during the sermon but won't speak to people in the hallway before and after church? Church can be such a crowd of selfish individualism rather than community of people seeking to love, grow and serve.

/27

You got to face it to fix it. You got to love it to live it. You got to care for it to keep it.

/28

Don't you just hate it when you know that today you're paying for yesterday's bad decision? Learn from it so that tomorrow will be spent reaching potential and not facing consequence.

MARCH

/01

Don't allow people who don't help complete your space to complicate it.

/02

Give someone who loves you a new reason to. Rest in love but don't rest on love. Let love flow and grow.

/03

No matter how long you all are together, win her daily!

/04

Wherever it applies, we need wisdom, courage, and strength to hold on, let go, or reach for.

/05

Tripbox: Maybe (just maybe) an American church system that produces and capitalizes on perpetually weak and needy Christians is a scheme of the devil. We are making few soldiers of the cross.

/06

Count on God to give you the tools, the team, and the time to get done what he has sent you to do.

/07

I want to see focus, passion, vision and sacrifice that are on a greater level than what's common and usual in human exchange. That's love. Does this deal with John 3:16?

/08

Plan for the pain in the process so that it doesn't surprise you or stop you.

/09

I hope you're not playing games in your relationships like The Price is Right, Jeopardy, Press Your Luck, The Weakest Link, or Solitaire.

/10

Don't break the heart you know for the body you're curious about.

/11

Don't live in fantasy. Know the facts even if you have to defy them. Walk by faith.

/12

When we are great by God's standard it's because we are serving with a sincere heart. When we achieve greatness on humanity's scale it's because of God's grace.

/13

I pray you are gifted, anointed, productive, loving, giving, happy, and ethical.
FIND YOUR GREAT!

/14

Be more. Do more. Have more. Give more. Learn more. Spend less. Save more.

/15

If you serve to be valuable you won't need to seek to be valued. Many people want to make a name for themselves without making a difference for others. Productivity > popularity.

/16

Love should never be an assumption. It should always be a conclusion. When asked if a person loves you, the answer should not be, "I guess".

/17

Have a standard and be ready to meet a standard. Her standards are as important as yours in real relationship.

/18

Better to be a little unsure, unclear and uncomfortable going somewhere with God than sure, clear, and comfortable going nowhere.

/19

My desire is to never disappoint God or fail the people I love. I don't always achieve what I desire.

/20

Let something move you to move something. Be motivated to get something done.

/21

Dream a big dream, build a great team, then go make your dream your reality no matter how impossible it seems.

/22

Peace is priceless. Don't disturb yours.

/23

Some people want companionship.
Others just want company. Make
sure your person wants a partner
and not just a supplier.

/24

If you're done, make an
announcement. Do not leave it to
her to draw a conclusion.

/25

Decide what you can't afford to loose. That will help you determine the choices you make and the chances you take.

/26

When you ask God to do something through you, the cause becomes more important than your comfort. "Lord have your way" may be more than what you bargained for.

/27

The goal now affects me more than the resistance.

/28

I hope the person you used to be is not better than the person you are now.

/29

You will never get to the next great moment if you don't keep going. Keep it moving.

/30

Never allow yourself to view your mate as an opponent even in an ongoing dispute. Fight for the relationship even when you're fighting with each other. Stay in each other's corner never the opposite corners. You remain close enough to see other stuff you love and not just what's getting on your nerves at the time.

/31

If you're dating and all you do is fight, then being with her is about your ego, the sex, control or some other illegitimate, dysfunctional reason. Love is not war.

APRIL

/01

Sometimes you have to let your dream interrupt your reality and refuse to let your present reality interfere with you making your dream come true.

/02

It's easy to get tired of church when there is not much Kingdom work being done.

/03

Be Healthy (Emotionally, Spiritually, Physically) Hopeful, and Happy. Passionately pursue and protect your wholeness.

/04

Positively concentrate on yourself. Self-discovery, self-awareness, self-development, self- maintenance, self- control, self-love, selflessness, self-sacrifice (the last two protect you from being selfish and self-absorbed). All should lead to self-assurance and true self-awareness.

/05

Whatever you can't get over will take you under. Let it go.

/06

Love's birthed. Love breathes. Love grows. Love feeds. Love's hurt. Love bleeds. Love's bandaged. Love heals. Love lives.

/07

Fellas stop playing in the shop if there is no intent to make a purchase.

/08

Don't allow yourself to feel good about becoming a "worse" you. Don't allow others to make you feel bad about becoming a "better" you.

/09

One day we will learn that holiness has fewer complications.

/10

Three questions:
1. Who have you decided to be?
2. What do you really want?
3. What's the very least God can consistently expect from you?

/11

For many it's time for better options, choices, and decisions. Output is directly tied to input.

/12

Holding on when you should be letting go will drag you down. Letting go when you should be holding on will do the same...

/13

Relationships (all kinds) are a risk. Alone is a definite loss. Family, friends, etc, go and love.

/14

Sir, you want a woman who requires you to check on her, not one you think you need to keep in check or whose actions compel you to check up on her. If you've got her, check on her as hard as you checked her out and chased her. And make sure you keep making that $ check and manage it well.

/15

This is a time to make key additions and strategic deletions. Adding often requires subtracting and subtraction can create addition.

/16

GOD can do INCREDIBLE work through us. WE must work to maintain our CREDIBILITY.

/17

What are your chances of being great today?

/18

Your decisions will affect you as much as your prayers.

/19

Say something nice, See something beautiful, Sow something into someone else, shake off the negative, Sit still and soak in God's love.

/20

I really hope your relationships are not like diapers, gas stations, and fast food restaurants...Disposable and messy, self service and expensive, unhealthy and drive through.

/21

Always appreciate her and provide emotional support. Remember all physical touch shouldn't be foreplay.

/22

There are mountains you speak to in order to remove them. There are other mountains you must climb. There are battles that are the Lord's. Then there are some you must fight. Knowing the difference can save a lot of time, effort, and energy.

/23

FARTHER, DEEPER, HIGHER!
Let's go!

/24

Don't judge yourself by your achievement. Judge yourself by your assignment that way you won't try to do more or settle for less than you should. By the way your chief assignment is to be like Jesus.

/25

Trust God. Face your fears, Meet the challenge. Win the battles. Celebrate the victory. Repeat.

/26

As you work on yourself make sure your empty spaces are not cracked or broken. If they are God can't fill them because they will leak, and God is not wasteful.

/27

Love awakened you and woke you up to go love. In part, God loves us thru us.

/28

There is not a woman alive who can put you on the straight and narrow. That's going to be a man's job. That man is you.

/29

When you don't have anything to say, be silent.

/30

If God is really on your side, then who cares who the star of your opposing team is. Stop worrying about him, her, or it.

MAY

/01

It's Monday.
You're alive.
Now what?

/02

You can't always trust your reflection alone. To see the real you, you need a mirror, a portrait, an action shot, and a trusted person's outside view.

/03

Make good decisions today.

/04

We learned in grammar school that a verb is an action word. LOVE is a VERB. That is all.

/05

When you learn to be a man people will see it. You won't have to announce it or try to prove it. Real manhood is obvious.

/06

Sometimes you have to do things people will appreciate you for later not just the things they will like you for now.

/07

Let God's will be your only limitation.

/08

Every day you have a chance. Some days you will have challenges. Focus on the chance.

/09

Some people struggle endlessly in life because they can't close the gap between their heart, head, and hand. Passions, thoughts, actions.

/10

Keep your heart open, your eyes too.

/11

Real love is work. It's a joy and pleasure but it's work. If you're not working, you're not loving.

/12

Sunday is Mother's Day. Does the way you treat women make your mother proud?

/13

What poverty and pain have created, prayer, love and resources must destroy. Counteract and neutralize poor decisions with good ones.

/14

Grace wins!

/15
FIND YOUR GREAT!

/16

Somewhere in your life you have or need 3 projects: a construction, a demolition, and a renovation. So get to work.

/17

Protect what you can't afford to lose. While it is possible to have an intense, temporary craving for the unimportant, the grief from the loss of something with actual importance is stronger and will potentially last longer than the desire for something insignificant.

/18

What a friend we have in Jesus... yes! But you're either too deep or really too relationally shallow if you have no other friends.

/19

You may not be able to fix what you didn't break. If someone or something else broke her you may have to wait until she heals.

/20

You didn't wake down.
You woke UP.
Let's go get it!

/21

Obedience is not extra. We don't get a bonus for obeying.

/22

Why don't you work with God to make your "I am" more prominent and powerful than your "I was".

/23

Decide what's RIGHT for you.
Distance yourself from what has to
be LEFT alone.

/24

Be open to God's voice and
direction. Commit to preparation.

Get started.

/25

Where are you in your relationship life? Satisfied and secure in what you have? Single and searching or waiting to be the end of the right person's search? Still recovering from the last situation? Salvaging what you have because you know its potential? Settling for what you can get? (be honest). Sharing or Sabotaging someone else's thing? (BE HONEST). Shut down and shutting everybody out?

/26

A woman can now be President for real. Raise your daughters accordingly.

/27

What you feed will grow. What you starve will not.

/28

Somehow an all-knowing God thought it was a good idea to love me. WOW! I could take that as an affirmation of my being, but I think it says more about Him than it does me.

/29

You cannot be bothered by everyone's opinion, but you do need to be open to honest critique.

/30

Courage. Character. Creativity. Care.
The right Course. The right Crew.
The correct Cause. Mix them as
needed.

/31

Don't try to seize what God didn't
say.

JUNE

/01

You will always need a friend.

/02

Don't keep yourself in position to have to be rescued by a woman. That includes your mother.

/03

There are sacrifices for which you can never be repaid but it's great when people show you they remember.

/04

The more God means to you the more his people will matter to you.

/05

There's a time to be daring. There's a time to show that you're stable. Press the issue. Push the envelope, but don't be reckless or impulsive.

/06

The obstacles will test how much you really want what you're pursuing.

/07

Do not miss your turn because it didn't come on your terms.

/08

Are you through being good to me?

/09

It's tough on her if you're a man who won't talk to her. If she is a woman you can't talk to, it is even worse for you.

/10

If you commit to the process you end up with the goal. If you refuse to commit to the process, then you don't want the goal as badly as you claim.

/11

God does send signals. Don't run the red lights. STOP! Don't sit at the green lights. GO! Your senses should let you know how to proceed with caution on the yellow lights.

/12

Live Your Life in the Active Voice. Be the subject not the object of the sentence of your life.

/13

Is there any reason not to be at your best?

/14

There is a difference between a challenge and a problem. Don't confuse the two.

/15

Unfortunately a relationship with a person can devolve from attraction, to boredom, to tolerance, to neglect, to borderline abuse. Don't just be along for a ride that could eventually end in a bad crash. Pay attention. Speak up. Think. Pray. Act.

/16

Be honest with yourself if you have found the one but you're not ready for only one. She can't make you ready for exclusivity.

/17

Part of the beauty of falling down
is the strength you discover while
getting up.

/18

God gives so that we can.

/19

See something. Be something. Do something. Start something. Stop something. Change something. Improve something. Make something happen...today. Or why get out of bed taking up space and time.

/20

It's easy to be critical. It's more helpful to be helpful.

/21

Keep working. Keep getting laughs where you can.

/22

If you did it wrong, do it over if you have the chance. If there is no chance to do it over, the best you can do is not do it again. That won't be good enough for some.

/23

If your lady has Daddy issues they will usually bleed over into your relationship. With that in mind if you have a daughter do your best to make sure she doesn't have Daddy issues.

/24

Pray. Love. Forgive. Live. Serve.

/25

Seek. Settle. Submit. Strive. May God direct us to spend our time and energy on what is meant to be not what we want to be.

/26

We all have a certain amount of days; the number of which we are uncertain. Don't waste. Commit. Connect. Prepare. Pursue. Learn. Love. Achieve. Allow. Enjoy. Empower. Have faith. Have fun.

/27

Will is always a greater factor than opportunity or knowledge. How many times have we said, "I shouldn't but I will!".

/28

You can make a difference. There is plenty of opportunity.

/29

People in your life should earn the right to say, "I love you." You shouldn't have to hear what they can't seem to consistently show.

/30

Grow to the point where you stop minimally investing yourself in a few women and start maximally investing yourself in the right One. The dividends are much greater.

JULY

/01

Have you seen you at your best lately?

/02

God often makes us successful by creating the proper tension between our strengths and our struggles.

/03

I want to matter in the matters that matter the most. Everything else is extra.

/04

You might know your ultimate goal, but have you mapped out your next move?

/05

Don't be dumb today.

/06

If it doesn't have to be a problem, don't let it be. Choose the relationship over a minor issue.

/07

A relationship with a good woman will inevitably require you to be a better man. You will always need to improve in some area that is directly tied to your partner's satisfaction and the success of the relationship. It's just the way it is.

/08

The Good news is the bad news didn't kill you. Keep fighting.

/09

God is not going to give you strength to climb something you're supposed to speak to.

/10

Are you praying or procrastinating? Decide and take the next step.

/11

Support your dreams. Wake up. Get up and make them come true.

/12

Did>Can. Action>Words. Deeds>Thoughts.

/13

Every action has eventual consequence. What you can do is a matter of ability and opportunity. What you should do is a matter of knowledge, morality and wisdom. What you will do is a matter of character, choice, and possibly constraints.

/14

If you decide what kind of man you want to be it will help you determine what kind of woman you need. There needs to be a match.

/15

Does it have to be convenient?

/16

Lord, for your glory and humanity's gain, give us the grace and the guts to be great.

/17

Never be so consumed with what you could have been that you don't have any energy left to work on what you can be.

/18

Life has so many twists and turns. Know when to be flexible. Know when not to be.

/19

Spend time. Don't waste it.

/20

Peace has no substitute.

/21

If her looks and what she does sexually are the only reasons she adds value to your life then one of you is with the wrong person. Either she's not the woman you need or you're not the man she needs. The same rule applies if she's only with you because you're her ATM.

/22

You may never know the most you can do until you determine the least you will do. You set the floor. God will set the ceiling.

/23

As America gets less and less humane. Christians have to be more and more Christ-like, that is loving, strong, sacrificial, merciful, principled, and transformational all at the same time. This is such a complicated mix only the Holy Spirit working through us can pull it off. It's dark. Where is the light?

/24

Sacrifice now so you won't have to suffer later!

/25

Fight for your smile today.

/26

It doesn't matter if the grass is greener if it's not your yard.

/27

Real love never just goes away. It lives on or it dies. If it dies and is not resurrected in time, bury it and go have some chicken at the repast. (You all know how we do. Lol)

/28

When you grow up, get a wife but not until. Marriage is for men not big boys.

/29

Real Vision for the future helps me to be completely present and accountable in my present. Grind in the now to get to the later.

/30

While you're waiting on your blessing, is there anything else you could be doing in the meantime? (Church people I know you're praising but is there something else. Haha).

/31

Your purpose is connected to people, but can only be negated by one person, YOU. Keep people around who will save you from self-sabotage.

AUGUST

/01

Don't you just hate it when you know that today you're paying for yesterday's bad decision? Learn from it so that tomorrow will be spent reaching potential and not facing consequence.

/02

Change is about where you're headed. Comfort is connected to where you've been. Discomfort is challenging, but the change might be worth it. #thechangeisworththechallenge

/03

Make a difference with your presence or make room with your absence.

/04

There are plenty of women to see when your eyes are open. What matters is whose face comes up when your eyes are closed. Your soul is talking.

/05

This is not the time to be dumb at anything that matters. Biblical, Financial, and/or Relational illiteracy or immaturity will cost you right now.

/06

Sometimes I'm amazed at what I'm capable of with God's help. Other times I'm amazed at what I'm capable of without God's spirit.

/07

When you decide to go to another level make sure it's not a lower level.

/08

Consequence can be a great teacher. Sometimes you can't skip her class.

/09

Decide what's important NOW so that you don't Discover it LATER and it's in poor condition because of neglect. (Uhh stuff like your health, marriage, your kids etc etc.

/10

When it comes to angry words, deviant actions, hormonal stimulated action (said that nicely lol), etc RESISTING is better than REGRETTING.

/11

You can't see her or touch her and she can't touch you. Now what is it that you love about her?

/12

Failure is only final when you make your last try your last try.

/13

God loves and cares for you, yet in some places and to some people (especially your family) you matter and in/to some you don't. Be okay with that.

/14

20 thoughts x 0 deeds = 0. In some cases it's not the thought that counts.

/15

If only we would think before we act or speak, so we wouldn't have to think about what we shouldn't have done or said.

/16

Make sure your life has the right combination of routine, risk, and realignment.

/17

Pretending to be real is being fake. Don't let people connect with who you're trying to be. Give them a chance to make a decision about the actual, present you and tell them about who you are trying to become. Maybe they can help you grow.

/18

Do you love her or are you caught up? The longer you're in the relationship the more you both will discover the difference.

/19

A great way to maintain your personal integrity is before you do something ask yourself, "Am I going to have to lie about this?"

/20

After we bow (worship) and kneel (pray), it's time to, sit (wait), stand (watch), walk (progress), run (accelerate), or soar (go to new dimensions). Discern which one. (Note) if it's time to soar don't miss your flight time.

/21

Constantly facing the challenges of life is not the same as consistently challenging yourself. The first is survival. The second is intentional growth.

/22

If the "never would" of your life has become "always" and the "always" have become "never do" you're either doing really good or really bad.

/23

Minimize regret. Don't allow your life to be filled with too many "I wish I had never" and so many "I wish I had". Take good risks. Stop taking bad ones.

/24

Sis,

You can be the perfect one and still not be the preferred one. It's just the way it is sometimes. Don't let it beat you down.

/25

Learn how to say no.

/26

Please don't just grow older. Grow up.

/27

I'm hearing a call to get better at love.

/28

Whoever said IT would be easy, lied. Whoever said IT is impossible lied too. You just have to be sure about IT.

/29

A good situation could be the secret to your success but remember bad habits will eventually catch up with you no matter how well things are presently going.

/30

Never say "Yes" with your mouth or your actions when your gut is screaming "No"

/31

I am trying to redefine what it means to have relationship, friendship or kinship. Whatever they are, I have concluded they are different than affinity, affection, or mere affiliation.

SEPTEMBER

/01

Be the president of her fan club and the main member of her support team.

/02

Why do so many people try to stand without trying to be outstanding?

/03

Extremely Gifted people should always remember that it's a GIFT and act accordingly. We need some more humility in the church world.

/04

It won't happen over night. It happens everyday. Be targeted and consistent.

/05

Life is a struggle, but the struggling shouldn't be perpetual or in the same place. It's time to expand and elevate. Let's go face the struggles in bigger places, on higher plains, and of greater impact and importance.

/06

Stop hanging out with people who are just hanging around. You cannot fulfill your purpose always around people who are not pursuing theirs.

/07

Which mistake are you most prone to: Loving the wrong person the right way or Loving right person the wrong way?

/08

Ladies, if your man is indecisive about where he's taking the relationship, tell him to kick rocks with open-toed shoes.

/09

Often transition presents this Catch 22 that keeps you paralyzed (stuck) and decision-less: Staying is damaging, but leaving is so difficult.

/10

No one should OVERsee if they do not know what it means to be truly UNDER authority.

/11

What's your next move? Is it one of these? Move Up (operate on a new level)? Move In (totally commit. Get settled in the new)? Move out (Separate from the past)? Move On (Advancement should follow liberation)? Move Something (make the effort)?

/12

The Natural can teach us stuff about the spiritual. When some pick up weight rather than working hard and losing it, they simply find something to effectively and even aesthetically cover it. What else have we learned to cover rather than get rid of?

/13

Wishing for it won't get as much done as working at it.

/14

How far is the gap between what you want to do and what you're willing to do? Depending on what the desire is you may have to work to either build a bridge or burn one.

/15

Learn what she likes. Also learn to detect what she needs. Some women just want you to pay. Most want you to pay attention as well.

/16

Happiness, laughter, enjoyment and recreation are not sins.

/17

Working on being even more gracious since I require so much grace.

/18

Are people you trust making a series of serious mistakes or are they starting to show you their true character?

/19

True Greatness seems to find the others of the same kind.

/20

If you commit to the process you end up with the goal. If you refuse to commit to the process, then you don't want the goal as badly as you claim.

/21

We need the Holy Ghost in order to love the way we are supposed to!

/22

If you're going to actively love someone forever, you will eventually have to forgive them for something.

/23

Goodness and mercy follow you, but just where are you going?

/24

Some people think it's victory when they get the last laugh on their enemy. I think victory is when they can find a way to smile together.

/25

Don't underestimate the God in you. Don't overestimate the you in you. You're good. God is great!

/26

Walking by faith requires fighting normal and natural emotions with a "right now" belief in the power of Jesus.

/27

Intend and contend. Do not pretend.

/28

Hold on when you should. Let go when you must. Progress and contentment will be found in some combination of the two.

/29

Women keep teaching me that one of the best things a man can do is to consistently do what he says he's going to do. Fellas, we have to focus on improving on that.

/30

Supposed to be -> will be ->
praying to be -> working to be ->
determined to be -> I Am!

OCTOBER

/01

Games can be won or lost in the 4th qtr. Where are you behind in your life? Fight hard. Finish strong. Win at the end.

/02

Faith is minute by minute, instance by instance. It is not easy at times.

/03

Avoid self-sabotage. Don't get in your own way today.

/04

Don't let self-promotion be so overwhelming that your product or performance cannot live up to it.

/05

You need some where I've been friends, some where I am friends and some where I'm going friends.

/06

Some people act a fool. Some people aren't acting.

/07

I got up to grow, create and serve.

/08

Your job is to say YES...His job is to do the rest!

/09

Be better today than you thought you could be yesterday.

/10

Some people want you to erase the past in order for them to embrace you in the present. Change is a matter for the present and the future. You can't change the past.

/11

Some things you didn't quit. You just finally stopped running red lights.

/12

Most people have unconsciously determined what they will say "yes" to. Have you consciously decided what you will always say "no" to?

/13

When it's time to change, CHANGE.

/14

The great ones learn their craft and know their stuff. Make it a practice to learn everything you need to and everything you can about that thing in which you are trying to be great.

/15

When our dreams die, we need something besides our emotions. We need the security of the scriptures.

/16

Education and knowledge (I prefer to call it know-how) are critical if you want be great.

/17

Choose wisely today.

/18

Remember, there could always
be something you don't like inside
something you love.

/19

Never allow yourself to view your mate as an opponent even in an ongoing dispute. Fight for the relationship even when you're fighting with each other.

/20

Determine who you love. Declare your love. Demonstrate love daily. Never let them doubt it or forget it.

/21

#startingandstopping.

There are some things I wish I had started earlier and some things I wish I had stopped sooner. There are some things I wish I had never started and some things I wish I had never stopped. Things not started are already stopped. Get started on the positive. Don't start the negative.

/22

If you allow Him, God will extend the requirements and demands of your life past your ability and create daily, total dependency on Him.

/23

There is something at which you're meant to be great! This has become a core belief of mine.

/24

Decide what's necessary.

/25

Mental toughness is the perseverance and passion to achieve long-term goals – that make a difference.

/26

Some days you long for the celebration of true love, but today you feel like reverting to your interpersonal isolation, tendency toward temporary/disposable relationships or unwillingness to work on your marriage. You can't have it both ways.

/27

Time will always tell if you are called to do it or if you just chose to do it. God allows choice but calling withstands what choice cannot.

/28

Why can't we remember that regaining something you shouldn't have lost can be tough. Discipline is actually easier than intervention.

/29

Do not let the failure of someone else to do his job cause you to move out of preparation season. We are held accountable for the season we are in. Watching unmet needs can draw you out of needed preparation if you're not careful.

/30

On far too many occasions we don't reach our peak potential or achieve our goals because of the lack of mental toughness.

/31

Greatness is not developed or achieved in a vacuum. It is directly connected to a set of circumstances. Anyone who is truly great serves others or solves issues.

NOVEMBER

/01

Yesterday's dream about tomorrow's success requires decisions and actions TODAY. Get to it.

/02

God made us relational. We have different kinds of relationships because we weren't built to be alone or at our best by ourselves.

/03

Is there a direct correlation between mama's boy and ladies' man? Does the former generally "graduate" to the latter if the process is not interrupted?

/04

#Tripbox.
The saints got to stop building and living in "spiritual" fantasy lands just because real life preparation, prayer, faith, endurance, real relationship building, decision making, discipline and courage are too hard.

/05

Knowing and accepting what God does not have for you is as important as knowing and embracing what God has for you. Embracing what he does have for you directs your time, energy, and resources. Accepting what he does not have for you keeps you from wasting time, energy, and resources.

/06

Based on the job you're doing for yourself right now, if you were a loved one would you hire you to take care of you? If not maybe you don't love you enough to give yourself good care.

/07

God doesn't always tell you ALL that you said yes too.

/08

Never forget that at the end of the day people are going to be well... people. Create emotional space for their failures so that disappointment and despair do minimal damage. And forever God will be God. He will not fail you even when he let's others fail you.

/09

Some people are missing. Some people are just absent. Missing is a statement of relationship and/or value. Absence is simply a statement of fact.

/10

I love you should come from the bottom of your heart and not the top of your head.

/11

There's nothing worse than shallow water calling itself deep.

/12

Being a living sacrifice will prevent you from becoming dead weight.

/13

Need can be revealing. The next time you're in spiritual, material or emotional need, it will unveil if you've made investments in others and if those investments were in the right people. Of course you will have one or two people who've got you regardless. If not you're really jacked. Lol

/14

It's difficult to build for tomorrow when you're still battling yesterday.

/15

Mental toughness is a character trait. It is not motivation, anointing or will. It is strength.

/16

Give someone who loves you a new reason to. Rest in love but don't rest on love. Let love flow and grow.

/17

A woman should know her intrinsic value. She determines her worth. We decide what she is worth to us.

/18

Make a suggestion of something fun to do this weekend to help enjoyment-challenged saints who simply pray, worship, go to work, do ministry, and take care of family responsibilities.

#helpforboringchristians

/19

God's grace, his favor and empowering presence, makes greatness possible. His grace is sufficient. You really do have the grace to be grace.

/20

I thought I was being excluded when actually I was being shielded. I was left out of what I could see so I could be kept out of what I couldn't see.

/21

Periodically you have to fight for you, your being, your psyche, your soul. Fight, but use the correct weapons against the right enemies. Fight!! But, be warned others may think you're fighting against them when you're just fighting for you. Provide understanding where you can and prayer where you can't but keep fighting.

/22

The director decides when you go center stage. The official decides when you start the race. Don't jump the gun.

/23

People who love you can accept "no" from you. Never think it's true or healthy love when it requires you to consistently say "yes", acquiesce or agree to get along.

/24

If you have the one worth your all, keep her. If you don't and you're single, look for her. If you don't and you're married, gently help make her so.

/25

The passion to prepare should be as great as the passion to perform. Preparation is not glamorous or glorious. Sometimes it is not even enjoyable. But, prepare yourself with the thought in mind that you are getting ready to solve problems and serve people. Grind it out.

/26

Sometimes when God takes the lead you don't end up in front, but if you're in his will you're still winning.

/27

On this next trip you cannot check luggage, so only pack what you can carry and still get to your destination on time.

/28

Some people will never learn. Don't you be one of them. Every experience is an education. Education helps you know what not to do.

/29

Sometimes there is just no point in saying what you think or feel regardless of how often you think it or strongly you feel it. Speak for results and not just release. Don't waste your breath.

/30

Leaders, spouses, and significant others, you should have a greater sense of responsibility when you know someone thanks God for YOU.

DECEMBER

/01

Don't commit to love if you don't love being committed.

/02

To be great at something you may have to be average or below at something else. Choose wisely.

/03

God broke the outer me to save the inner me.

/04

Excellence is a daily habit.

/05

I decided not to show up for the funeral my enemies had planned for me.

/06

Your doubt or disagreement doesn't create confusion for me. I yet believe.

/07

Your lover can do more damage to you than your haters. Choose wisely.

/08

Two words that are difficult to recover from:

She's Gone.

/09

I discovered I did not have a life. I had a routine. They are not the same.

/10

Honor God. Fulfill your responsibilities. Develop into your best self. Help humanity. Have fun. Do what you love. Be with who you love. Have no conflicts between any of the above. This about sizes up a pretty good life.

/11

Imagine what it would be like to be your happiest and most productive and to also be at peace. Now dedicate yourself to it and let nothing stop you.

/12

There is long term regret ahead of you when you don't understand and/or respect when you're in a "can't blow this" moment or season.

/13

Develop healthy habits. They will get you further than any resolution. Soldiers are taught to rely on their training while in combat. Be a trained soldier in the army of the Lord.

/14

When you begin negotiating with what should be non-negotiable you enter a level of compromise that can cause you to lose your best self.

/15

Do not take away her ability to always give you the benefit of the doubt. Maintain her ability to blindly trust you.

/16

It doesn't matter the situation (the economy) if mentality and habits don't change. It's funny that many of us will spend money we shouldn't (management) or we don't have (debt) because it's Christmas. So some are going into debt in Jesus' name. Funny.

/17

Whatever you can't praise Him for you should not participate in.

/18

Preparation is properly managing today's effect on tomorrow. As I've said for years, when it's time to prepare, prepare for when it's time to produce you won't have time to prepare.

/19

Every single day winning, enjoying the win, in the process of winning, planning a winning strategy or resting.

/20

I'm not always clear on the path, the partners, or the process but I am crystal clear on the destination. The finish line is to be like Jesus. May Christ be formed in me.

/21

Two short sentences with endless implications:

I love you.
I promise.

/22

Never blow your opportunity (single fellas) or the sheer joy (married fellas) of daily waking up to the woman you dream about at night. Protect the irreplaceable.

/23

Some of us have too many things
and people pulling on us, and not
enough of them pushing us.

/24

Christianity is about keys. Too many
make it about locks and chains.

/25

I lost some people this year. I'm taking the hit. Some people lost me this year. They are taking the hit. In some cases we both broke even. In the future it could be a gain for both parties.

/26

It's the day after Christmas, the day for returns and exchanges. If only the rest of life was so simple. IT'S NOT, so choose wisely and be careful what you accept and from whom you accept it. You could get stuck with it.

/27

I choose to live my life with my dreams affecting my reality rather than my reality affecting my dreams.

/28

Never sacrifice relationships meant to be long-term on the altar of a short-term emotion, situation, need or impulse.

/29

Find the woman that makes you wink, think, blink, and work out your kinks.

/30

What good are resolutions if there is no accountability for results? Declarations without duty or commitments without consequence won't matter in a month.

/31

A New Year won't cure old Patterns of living. HOW you are will be connected to WHO you are. (Change position of the "w". Soul Train Scramble Board. Lol.)

#haveahappynewyou

43894521R00117